Away in a Manger

An ABC Book on the Birth of Jesus Christ

Written by Cindy Brouse Kenealy
and Illustrated by Martha Reppert

AuthorHouse™
1663 Liberty Drive
Bloomington, IN 47403
www.authorhouse.com
Phone: 1-800-839-8640

First published by AuthorHouse 2/18/2011

ISBN: 978-1-4520-2293-2 (sc)

Library of Congress Control Number: 2010907221

Printed in the United States of America
Bloomington, Indiana

This book is printed on acid-free paper.

authorHOUSE®

This book is dedicated to Jonathan and Benjamin, my sons.
You two are the joy of my life.
May your lives always shine with the love of our Savior.

Cindy Brouse Kenealy

The pictures in this book are dedicated to Scott and Andrew.
My sons, my love, my life.

Martha Reppert

*A*way in a manger, the story is told;

The birth of our Savior did unfold.

Luke 2:11 Today in the town of David, a Savior has been born to you; he is Christ the Lord.

Far away from their home,

To Bethlehem they did roam.

Luke2:4 So Joseph also went up from the town of Nazareth in Galilee to Judea, to Bethlehem the town of David.

The Census was a government demand

Declared across the entire land.

Luke 2:1 In those days, Caesar Augustus issued a decree that a census should be taken of the entire Roman world.

The Donkey's heart was filled with pride,

Carrying Mary, with Joseph walking at her side.

Luke 2:3 And everyone went to his own town to register.

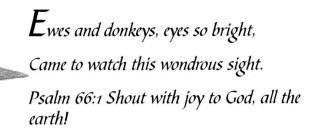

*E*wes and donkeys, eyes so bright,

Came to watch this wondrous sight.

Psalm 66:1 Shout with joy to God, all the earth!

*F*rankincense for the King;

A gift the wise men they did bring.

Matthew 2:11 On coming to the house, they saw the child with his mother Mary, and they bowed down and worshiped him.

Shiny *G*old they also gave,

And Myrrh, a symbol that Jesus would save.

Matthew 2:11 Then they opened their treasures and presented him with gifts of gold and of incense and of myrrh.

*H*erod's rule caused an outcry;

Baby boys were ordered to die.

Matthew 2:16 When Herod realized that he had been outwitted by the Magi, he was furious, and he gave orders to kill all the boys in Bethlehem and its vicinity who were two years old and under, in accordance with the time he had learned from the Magi.

An *I*nn for weary Mary to rest?

No—only a stable was Joseph's best.

Luke 2:6-7 While they were there, the time came for the baby to be born, and she gave birth to her firstborn, a son. She wrapped him in clothes and placed him in a manger, because there was no room for them in the inn.

Joy to the world God did give;

He gave His only son so we might live.

John 3:16 For God so loved the world that He gave his one and only Son, that whoever believes in him shall not perish but have eternal life.

Jesus is the King of Kings;

Salvation for all, this new King brings.

Matthew 1:21 She will give birth to a son, and you are to give him the name Jesus, because he will save his people from their sins.

*L*anterns burning in the night;

Behold the Savior—a blessed sight.

Luke 2:11 Today in the town of David, a Savior has been born to you; he is Christ the Lord.

Blessed Mary, Virgin Mother,

God chose her above all others.

Luke 1:30 But the angel said to her, "Do not be afraid, Mary, you have found favor with God."

He'd be raised in Nazareth, this baby boy,

Filling his parents' hearts with love and joy.

Luke 2:13 When Joseph and Mary had done everything required by the Law of the Lord, they returned to Galilee to their own town of Nazareth. And the child grew and became strong; he was filled with wisdom, and the grace of God was upon him.

One bright and shiny little star

Guided the wise men from afar.

Matthew 2:1 After Jesus was born in Bethlehem in Judea, during the time of King Herod, Magi from the east came to Jerusalem and asked, "Where is the one who has been born king of the Jews? We saw the star in the east and have come to worship him."

Prophets told of God's only son

Coming to be king of everyone.

Luke 1:76 And you, my child, will be called a prophet of the Most High; for you will go on before the Lord to prepare the way for him, to give his people the knowledge of salvation through the forgiveness of their sins.

Quietly sleeping, this little one,

Mary knew in her heart he was God's son.

Luke 1:31-31 You will be with child and give birth to a son, and you are to give him the name Jesus. He will be great and will be called the Son of the Most High.

An angel **R**ejoicing from heaven above

Gave news to the shepherds of God's infinite love.

Luke 2: 9 An angel of the Lord appeared to them, and the glory of the Lord shone around them, and they were terrified.

Shepherds in their fields at night

Also saw the wondrous light.

Luke 2:8 And there were shepherds living out in the fields nearby, keeping watch over their flocks at night.

Tidings of comfort and joy

Celebrate the birth of this baby boy.

Luke 2:10 But the angel said to them, "Do not be afraid. I bring you good news of great joy that will be for all the people."

*U*pon the golden hay piled high

Did the baby Jesus lie.

Matthew 2:7 And she gave birth to her firstborn, a son. She wrapped him in cloths and placed him in a manger, because there was no room for them in the inn.

Hope filled the V*irgin Mary's heart*

With news the angels did impart.

Luke 2:19 Mary treasured up all these things and pondered them in her heart.

Wise men that came to worship and pray

Were warned to go home a different way.

Matthew 2:12 And having been warned in a dream not to go back to Herod, they returned to their country by another route.

*Angels sing in e**X**altation;*

Christ is born for all creation.

Luke 2:13-14 Suddenly, a great company of the heavenly host appeared with the angel, praising God and saying, "Glory to God in the highest, and on earth peace to men on whom his favor rests."

Yonder star burning bright,

Guide us to the babe tonight.

Matthew 2:9 After they had heard the king, they went on their way, and the star they had seen in the east went ahead of them until it stopped over the place where the child was.

Zeal for life the Savior's promise too.

He's coming again for me and you.

Revelation 1:7 Look, he is coming with the clouds, and every eye will see him, even those who pierced him; and all the peoples of the earth will mourn because of him. So shall it be!

A to *Z* is his story.

He'll come again in all His glory.

Revelation 21:6 He said to me: "It is done. I am the Alpha and the Omega, the Beginning and the End."

Glossary To Go with Letters

A – Scholars believe baby Jesus was laid in a manger. A manger is an animal's feeding trough. Mangers during that time were usually carved from stone and measured three to four feet in length. The cavity that held the food for animals would be just the right height for holding a baby.

B – Mary and Joseph traveled south from their home in Nazareth to Joseph's ancestral home of Bethlehem. King David was also born in Bethlehem (1 Samuel 16:1), and therefore Bethlehem is called the "City of David."

C – A census is the counting of people. This census was ordered by Caesar Augustus, better known as Octavian.

D – Mary and Joseph traveled by way of donkey to Bethlehem. It was about eighty miles and would have taken them three days to make this journey.

E – A ewe is a female sheep.

F – Frankincense comes from a deciduous tree and is used for incense. Giving a gift of frankincense was a symbolic gesture to recognize royalty and divinity.

G – Gold was symbolic of the infant's royalty. Myrrh makes reference to His future death. Myrrh was very valuable in the time of the Roman Empire, when Jesus was born, and was used as incense to burn during funerals.

H – Herod, king of Judea, held a meeting with the wise men. He asked them to report to him and share the whereabouts of the baby Jesus so that he too could worship the new "king." This was a lie. Herod was afraid he would be replaced as king of Judea by Jesus. When the wise men did not return to him, Herod ordered the death of all male children of Bethlehem under the age of two, thinking Jesus would certainly be one of the ones killed.

I – Bethlehem was very crowded when Mary and Joseph arrived because of the census. Luke 2 says there was no room for Mary and Joseph in the "inn." The Greek term translated for inn (kataluma) has multiple meanings. Some scholars believe that Mary and Joseph stayed not in an exterior stable, but inside the house in one of the ground floor rooms where animals were protected from the weather and thieves.

J – The birth of Jesus was an amazing event that fulfilled many scriptures. However, the greatest story and joy comes from knowing that Jesus gave his life on the cross so that all people might have eternal life.

K – Isaiah 9:6-7 tells of a child being born that will reign on David's throne and over his kingdom, upholding it with justice and righteousness from that time on and forever.

L – A lantern was used to protect the flame that produced light during this time period.

M – Mary was chosen by God to be the mother of Jesus.

N – Nazareth is the childhood home of Jesus. It is in Nazareth that Jesus learned the carpentry trade from Joseph.

O – The star that guided the wise men to Jesus is often referred to as the "Star of Bethlehem."

P – Prophets are people who foretell events and revelations of God's will.

Q – It was revealed to Mary by an angel that she would give birth to a baby and his name would be Jesus.

R – The first announcement of Christ's birth was sent by an angel to shepherds in a field at night. Scripture then tells of a host of angels appearing.

S – Shepherds' duties did not end with the sunset. Shepherds guarded their fold through the dark hours from the attack of wild animals or the attempts of thieves. In biblical times, society did not give much respect to the job of a shepherd. It was to these humble shepherds in their fields that the birth of Jesus was first announced.

T – Tidings are another way of saying or giving news.

U –The Bible says that after Jesus was born he was wrapped in swaddling cloth and laid in a manger. Swaddling clothes described in the Bible consisted of a cloth tied together by bandage-like strips. These strips kept the baby warm and also ensured that the child's limbs would grow straight.

V – Virgin refers to the fact that Mary was pure and specially chosen by God.

W – The Bible does not mention how many wise men there were. It is believed that there were three wise men since they came bearing three gifts for Jesus. In the book of Matthew, we learn of the dream the wise men received from God warning them not to go back to Herod. Consequently, they returned to their own country by another route.

X – Exultation means to rejoice exceedingly and to triumph.

Y – Yonder is a way of saying at a distance or far away. The wise men were described as coming from yonder.

Z – Zeal is a term used to describe intense enthusiasm for an event.

Printed in the United States
By Bookmasters